I ~~Don't~~ Matter

Yo ~~*No*~~ *Importo*

Written by Georgette Baker

Illustrations by Esther Holzmeister

Published by CANTEMOS ©2016 all rights reserved

Original story and translation by Georgette Baker

Artwork by Esther Holzmeister

No portion of this story may be copied or reproduced in any format without the written consent of the author.

Email author at : jarjetb@writeme.com

What's the matter Manny?

¿Qué te pasa Mani?

I don't matter to anybody.

No le importo a nadie.

Oh

O

Thanks Nana.

Gracias Nana.

 I wish I had a grandma to make me cookies.

Me gustaría tener una abuela para hacerme galletitas.

Manny. Come here, you received a card from your Aunt Dee.

Mani....

Ven acá, recibiste una carta de tu tía Dee.

What does it say?

¿Qué dice?

"To a special boy who I miss seeing"

"Para un niño especial a quien extraño"

Wow!

I have never gotten a card in the mail!

Uao!

¡Yo nunca he recibido una carta por correo!

Want to play ball, sonny?

¿Quieres jugar a la pelota, m'ijo?

Uh... nah Grampa, thanks.

Ah... no, abuelo, gracias.

My grandpa never plays with me.
Don't you like playing ball?

Mi abuelo nunca juega conmigo.
¿No te gusta jugar a la pelota?

Thanks Mom, I'll put them on.

Gracias Mami, me los pondré.

What is wrong Manny?

I don't matter.

¿Qué te pasa Mani?

Yo no importo.

To whom don't you matter?

Dad

Oh. Where is he?

Dunno

Is he coming back?

Dunno

¿A quién no le importas?

Papá

O. ¿Dónde esta?

No sé

¿Va a regresar?

No sé

Do you miss him?

Yes, no, dunno.

¿Lo extrañas?

Sí, no, no sé.

My Grandma says,

we need to count our blessings.

Mi abuelita dice que tenemos que contar

a nuestras bendiciones.

I DO MATTER!

¡YO SI IMPORTO!

Follow-up Questions

You matter, we all matter.

There are no wrong answers to any of these questions. They give the reader and the listener an opportunity to interact, share, grieve and have a say.

1. Why is Manny sad?

2. Where do you think Manny's father is?

3. Why do YOU think Manny's father hasn't returned?

4. Does Manny love his father?

5. Do you think Manny's father loves him?

6. What makes you think that?

7. What does "Count your blessings" mean?

8. Name some of Manny's blessings.

9. Why doesn't Manny see all the good things in his life at the beginning of the story?

10. What are the good things and "blessings" in your life that you are thankful for?

11. Does Manny matter as a person?

12. Do you sometimes feel that you don't matter?

13. Just because he FEELS he doesn't matter, does it mean it is true?

14. How does Manny's friend help him change his paradigm (the way he sees his life)?

15. Did Manny change quickly from sad to happy?

16. Can anyone change the way they see things and change their attitude and their life? What makes you say that?

17. Did Manny only think about himself and not about the people in his life?

18. Does Manny's friend wish for things she doesn't have? Why isn't she sad?

19. Do you think that anyone can be happy with what they have?

No hay respuestas incorrectas a estas preguntas. Le dan al lector y al oyente la oportunidad de interactuar, compartir, llorar y tener voz.

1.¿Por qué está triste Mani?

2.¿Dónde crees que está el papá de Mani?

3. ¿Por qué crees que el papá de Mani no ha regresado?

4. ¿Crees que Mani quiere a su papá ?

5.¿Cree que el papá de Manny lo quiere ? ¿Qué te hace pensar eso?

6. ¿Qué significa "Cuenta tus bendiciones" ?

7. Nombra algunas de las bendiciones de Mani.

8 ¿Por qué Mani no ve a todas las cosas buenas en su vida al comienzo del cuento?

9 ¿Cuáles son las cosas buenas y las "bendiciones" en TU vida por las cuales estás agradecido?

10. ¿Importa Mani como persona?

11.¿A veces sientes que no importas?

12. El hecho de que él se SIENTE que no importa, ¿quiere decir que es verdad?

13.¿Como ayuda la amiga de Mani a cambiar su paradigma (la forma en que el ve a su vida)?

14. ¿Crees que Mani cambió rápidamente de infeliz a feliz?

15. ¿Piensas que alguien puede cambiar su forma de ver las cosas y cambiar su actitud y su vida? ¿Qué te hace pensar eso?

16. ¿Piensas que Mani sólo piensa en sí mismo y no sobre la gente en su vida?

17. ¿Desea la amiga de Mani cosas que no tiene? Por qué no está triste?

18. ¿Piensas que cualquier persona puede ser feliz con lo que tiene?

BOOKS AND CD'S WRITTEN BY GEORGETTE BAKER available on amazon.com   email: bakergeorgette@yahoo

Http://www.cantemosco.com   Http://www.simplespanishsongs.com

- Aesop's Fables/Las Fabulas...
- Aluminum Castles
- Andi y la Mina de Oro
- Andy and the Gold Mine
- CANCIONES INFANTILES...
- Canciones Infantiles/Spanish...
- Castillos de Aluminio
- Children's Author Presentation Handbook
- Cuentos y Canciones/ Stories...
- Funics! Phonemic Awareness...
- Hallacas Venezolanas
- Las Fábulas de Ésopo
- Multicultural Stories
- Multicultural Stories/Cuentos...
- Patriotic American...
- Periquito
- Sandwiched
- Settle Down Sounds
- Sonidos Serenos
- TAGALOG Made Easy
- The Baby Manual
- We're Off to the Galapagos
- WE're Off...to Australia's Great...
- We're Off...to Kenya
- We're Off...to Learn Some...
- We're Off...to Mo'orea
- We're Off...to Peru

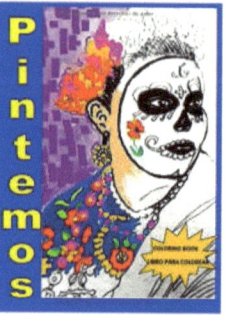

www.ingramcontent.com/pod-product-compliance
Lightning Source LLC
Chambersburg PA
CBHW041504220426
43661CB00016B/1247